PHILLIS *Wheatley*

SPIRIT
of America®

PHILLIS *Wheatley*

FIRST PUBLISHED AFRICAN-AMERICAN POET

By Deborah Kent

Content Adviser: Robert Hall, Museum Educator, Washington, D.C.

The Child's World®
The Child's World®
Chanhassen, Minnesota

PHILLIS *Wheatley*

Published in the United States of America by The Child's World®
PO Box 326 • Chanhassen, MN 55317-0326 • 800-599-READ • www.childsworld.com

Acknowledgments
   The Child's World®: Mary Berendes, Publishing Director

   Editorial Directions, Inc.: E. Russell Primm, Editorial Director; Pam Rosenberg, Line Editor; Elizabeth K. Martin, Assistant Editor; Olivia
   Nellums, Editorial Assistant; Susan Hindman, Copy Editor; Susan Ashley, Halley Gatenby, Proofreaders; Jean Cotterell, Kevin Cunningham,
   Peter Garnham, Fact Checkers; Tim Griffin/IndexServ, Indexer; Dawn Friedman, Photo Researcher; Linda S. Koutris, Photo Selector

Photo
   Cover: Stock Montage, Inc.; Angela Rowlings/AP/Wide World Photos: 27; copyright Elizabeth Catlett/licensed by VAGA, New York,
   NY/Cincinnati Art Museum: 28; Bettmann/Corbis: 7, 9, 11 bottom, 13, 16; Lee Snider/Corbis: 10; Michael Maslan Historic
   Photographs/Corbis: 11 top; Corbis: 12, 23 bottom; Museum of the City of New York/Corbis: 17; Historical Picture Archive/Corbis: 21;
   Kevin Fleming/Corbis: 26; The Granger Collection, New York: 25; Hulton Archive/Getty Images: 8, 15, 19, 23 top, 24; Courtesy of the
   Massachusetts Historical Society, MHS image #2168: 6; North Wind Picture Archives: 14; Photographs and Prints Division, Schomburg
   Center for Research in Black Culture, The New York Public Library, Astor, Lenox and Tilden Foundations: 18, 22; Stock Montage, Inc.: 2.

Registration

Library of Congress Cataloging-in-Publication Data
   Kent, Deborah.
    Phillis Wheatley : first published African-American poet / by Deborah Kent.
       p. cm. — (Our people)
   "Spirit of America series."
   Includes bibliographical references and index.
   Contents: The Wheatleys' wonder child—Poems on various subjects—Year of sorrow—
   Phillis Wheatley's legacy—Timeline.
    ISBN 1-59296-009-X (Library Bound : alk. paper)
    1. Wheatley, Phillis, 1753–1784—Juvenile literature. 2. Poets, American—
   Colonial period, ca. 1600–1775—Biography—Juvenile literature. 3. African American
   women poets—Biography—Juvenile literature. 4. Slaves—United States—Biography—
   Juvenile literature. 5. African American poets—Biography—Juvenile literature. [1. Wheatley,
   Phillis, 1753–1784. 2. Poets, American. 3. Women—Biography. 4. African Americans—Biography.] I. Title. II. Series.
    PS866.W5Z637 2004
    811'.1—dc21   2003004258

13   18   26

Contents

Chapter ONE

The Wheatleys' Wonder Child

A poem handwritten by Phillis Wheatley

A poem handwritten by Phillis Wheatley

AT AN AUCTION IN 1998, A RICH NEW YORKER bought the original **manuscript** of a poem called "Ocean." The pages were wrinkled and yellowed with age, but the buyer paid a whopping $68,500 for it. The poem had great historical value. "Ocean" was written by poet Phillis Wheatley, the first African-American writer to ever publish a book.

No one knows the name that Phillis Wheatley's parents gave her. No marker honors her birthplace. She was born somewhere in West Africa, probably in present-day Senegal, in about 1753. In 1761, slave hunters kidnapped her from her village. We can only imagine her terror as rough men, speaking a strange language, loaded her onto a ship. For weeks, she tossed on the waves with hundreds of other captives, sick, hungry, and afraid.

The ship's first **port of call** was an island in the West Indies. There, the healthiest, strongest captives were unloaded like cargo. They were sold as slaves to work in the sugarcane fields. The little girl from Senegal was too thin and weak for heavy labor. She and the remaining captives, mostly women and children, sailed on to Boston.

Boston was a thriving New England seaport in 1761, a center for trade and culture. Many families had servants to cook and clean house for them. Some of those servants were enslaved. A rich Boston tailor named John Wheatley bought the little girl from Senegal. She was thin and sickly, but he thought she could make a good house servant for his wife, Susannah. When he saw her in the slave market the girl wore no clothes, and was wrapped only in a piece of rug. The Wheatleys named

Hundreds of captives from Africa were loaded onto slave ships and brought to North America to be sold as slaves.

7

Interesting Fact

▶ Phillis Wheatley learned quickly. John Wheatley said that she mastered the English language within 16 months.

the girl Phillis, after the slave ship that brought her from Africa. John Wheatley guessed that Phillis was seven or eight years old because she was missing her two front teeth.

Within a few months, Phillis learned to speak English **fluently.** Sometimes she tried to copy letters on the wall with bits of chalk. The Wheatleys soon realized that she was very bright, and they took a special interest in her. They treated her more like a member of the family than a person who was enslaved. The Wheatley children, Mary and Nathaniel, taught Phillis to read and write. The Wheatleys introduced Phillis to the Bible, and she decided to become a Christian.

Phillis was hungry to learn, and the Wheatleys were eager to teach her. John Wheatley had a large collection of books. He let Phillis read anything

Slave traders inspect an African captive

she chose. She studied history, geography, and astronomy. She read famous English poets such as John Milton and Alexander Pope. She also studied Greek and Latin. The **myths** and legends of ancient Greece fired her imagination.

John Milton was an English poet. Phillis Wheatley studied his work.

Few servants, enslaved or free, ever learned to read. In many places in the United States, it was against the law for enslaved African-Americans to read. Not many girls, even the daughters of wealthy families, gained an education. Yet Phillis Wheatley, an enslaved girl from Africa, became one of the most learned young women in Boston. The Wheatleys were thrilled with her achievements. When visitors came, Phillis was called in to recite in Latin or to answer questions about Greek **philosophy.** Some guests were amazed and applauded. Others went away shaking their heads, sure that somehow they were being tricked. They couldn't believe that an enslaved girl could learn so much.

This building is located in Newport, Rhode Island. The Newport Mercury *newspaper in Newport published one of Wheatley's poems in 1767.*

When she was 13, Phillis began to write poetry. The Wheatleys offered her all the encouragement they could. They made sure she had plenty of paper, and they gave her extra candles so she could write late at night. In 1767, when Phillis was about 14, one of her poems was published in the *Newport Mercury* newspaper in Newport, Rhode Island. The poem described two sailors who had nearly drowned. Phillis praised God for sparing their lives. In the years that followed, the Wheatleys and their friends often asked Phillis to write poems marking special occasions. Many of her verses were written in memory of someone who had died. They were read at the funeral.

By the time she was 19, Phillis had written enough poems to fill a small book. The Wheatleys thought her work should be published. But finding a publisher for their amazing young African-American poet was far more difficult than they expected.

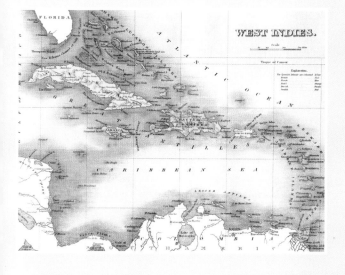

DURING THE 1700S, EUROPEANS used the triangular trade route to make money from the sale of enslaved Africans.

It was big business. The merchant ships sailed from Europe to Africa, from Africa to the Americas, and from the Americas back to Europe. Africans were captured, chained together, and forced to travel on these ships. The largest market for enslaved Africans was in the West Indies part of the Americas, where they worked on sugarcane plantations.

When the slave merchants reached the West Indies from Africa, they traded enslaved Africans for sugar, in the form of molasses. They then sold the molasses in New England, where it was used to make rum. The slave merchants used some of their profits to buy barrels of rum, glass beads, guns, and tobacco, which they took back to Europe. From Europe, men returned to Africa to once again participate in the triangular slave trade.

11

Chapter Two

Poems on Various Subjects

Many Boston publishing companies refused to publish Phillis Wheatley's work.

JOHN AND SUSANNAH WHEATLEY TOOK Phillis's poems to one Boston publisher after another. The publishers agreed that the poems were very well written. In fact, they said the poems were so good they could not possibly be Phillis's own work. No enslaved African girl could write such beautiful verses! The publishers thought the poems were a **hoax.** They refused to publish any of Phillis's work.

All over Boston, people argued about the Wheatleys and their enslaved girl. Was Phillis an **impostor?** Or was she a highly talented young woman

John Hancock was one of the men who tested Wheatley's knowledge.

with a splendid education, as her masters claimed? At last, a group of Boston's leading citizens decided to settle the matter once and for all.

In 1772, Phillis Wheatley faced the test of a lifetime. She stood before a group of 18 men, the most powerful merchants, ministers, and politicians in Boston. One of them was John Hancock, who later signed the Declara-

Interesting Fact

▶ Most of Phillis Wheatley's best-known poems were written before she was 20 years old.

13

tion of Independence. Another was Thomas Hutchinson, governor of the Massachusetts Colony. The men bombarded Phillis with questions about history and literature. They asked her to translate difficult passages from Greek and Latin. Again and again, they tried to disprove her claim to knowledge. Phillis answered their questions calmly, bravely, and correctly.

Thomas Hutchinson was the governor of the Massachusetts Colony and a member of the group of men who tested Wheatley's knowledge.

The 18 men were so impressed by her answers that they wrote a short **preface** to her still unpublished book: "We whose names are underwritten, do assure the world that the poems specified in the following pages were written by Phillis, a young Negro girl. … She has been examined by some of the best judges, and is thought qualified to write them."

Despite this strong statement from the judges, the Boston publishers still refused to produce Phillis's work. Susannah Wheatley wrote to a friend in London, the Countess of Huntington. She asked the countess to help find a London publisher for Phillis's poetry. The countess promised to do everything she could.

In the summer of 1773, Phillis sailed for England. Nathaniel Wheatley went with her. As the ship tossed on the waves, surely Phillis remembered her terrifying voyage from Africa. This trip was very different. She was no longer a frightened little girl, hungry and uncertain about her

Ships on the River Thames in London

future. Now she was a poet on her way to meet a countess. All the same, she was still enslaved. She belonged to John and Susannah Wheatley.

The Countess of Huntington introduced Phillis to many wealthy people. They treated

Just before her death, Susannah Wheatley signed manumission papers that made Phillis Wheatley a free woman.

the young African poet as a celebrity. Phillis went to parties and balls. She may even have met the king. A British publisher agreed to produce her book, which contained thirty-nine poems. The title was *Poems on Various Subjects, Religious and Moral.* Phillis dedicated the book to the Countess of Huntington, who had been so helpful to her.

Phillis had no time to rejoice. Before her book was published, she received word that Susannah Wheatley was gravely ill. Phillis hastily sailed back to Boston. For the next several months, she was Susannah's devoted nurse and companion. Susannah knew she would not live much longer. Before she died, she signed **manumission** papers for Phillis. Phillis Wheatley was a free woman at last.

16

IN 1772, MASSACHUSETTS WAS ONE OF 13 BRITISH COLONIES IN NORTH AMERICA. The colonies belonged to England, which was known as the mother country. The first British colony in North America was Virginia, founded in 1607.

Fighting broke out between the British and the American colonists in 1775. The colonists were angry about taxes and trade regulations imposed on them by the British government. At first, the colonists did not plan on breaking away from Great Britain. They were just fighting for the right to fair representation in the British government. But as the fighting continued, many colonists came to believe that the best course of action was to declare their independence from Great Britain.

In 1776, representatives from each of the colonies signed the Declaration of Independence. This announced that the colonies no longer accepted British rule. They now considered themselves to be the United States of America. The Revolutionary War continued until 1783. The United States won the war and was recognized as an independent nation.

Chapter THREE

Years of Sorrow

*A portrait of
Phillis Wheatley*

A FEW MONTHS AFTER HER MANU-
mission, Phillis sent a letter to her
friend Samson Occom. He was a
preacher who was a member of
the Mohican Indian tribe. "In
every human breast, God has
implanted a principle, which we
call love of freedom," she wrote.
"It is impatient of oppression, and
pants for deliverance."

Soon after the death of Susannah Wheatley, John Wheatley
and his daughter Mary also died.
Nathaniel Wheatley had married and was
now living in England. The Boston family
that had cared for Phillis and educated her
so eagerly was gone. Phillis was on her own.

18

Over the next several years, Phillis continued to write poetry. Many of her poems were published in newspapers or as small pamphlets. She was the most famous poet of the American colonies.

In 1778, when she was about 25, Phillis Wheatley married a free black man named John Peters. Peters was a grocer, but he did not do well in business. In fact, some records suggest that he was sent to prison for failing

The Boston Gazette *was one of the newspapers published in Boston during Phillis Wheatley's lifetime.*

Interesting Fact

Phillis Wheatley supported the American Revolutionary War and greatly admired George Washington. She wrote a poem in his honor and may have met him.

to pay his debts. As Peters's wife, Wheatley lived in poverty. The woman who had once dined with royalty now went to bed hungry night after night.

After her marriage to John Peters, Phillis Wheatley continued writing poetry. In 1779, she placed notices in two Boston newspapers, seeking a publisher for a second book. The new volume would contain 33 poems and 13 letters. Unfortunately, the book was never published. Under the name Phillis Peters, Wheatley published few poems about the American Revolution in 1784.

Phillis Wheatley and John Peters had three children. For a time, Wheatley and her children lived in a rundown boarding house for African-Americans. Two of the children died as infants. In 1784, Wheatley and her third child fell sick. On December 5, both mother and child died. Phillis Wheatley is buried in Boston in an unmarked grave along with her third child.

Shortly after his wife's death, John Peters visited the widowed niece of Susannah Wheatley, with whom Phillis and the children had lived briefly. Susannah Wheatley's niece

had the only copy of Wheatley's unpublished volume of poetry. She gave the manuscript to Peters and no one knows what became of it afterwards.

Many of Wheatley's poems celebrate her deep Christian faith. She writes of finding

In the 1700s, debtors were often sent to prisons or workhouses like this one when they were unable to pay what they owed.

true freedom in heaven after the hardships of life on earth. As she lay on her deathbed at the young age of about 31, perhaps Phillis Wheatley found comfort in her religious beliefs. Perhaps she looked forward to a new life in a far better world.

Phillis Wheatley was a young woman when she died.

DURING THE 1600S AND 1700S, many people believed that debtors—people who owed money to others and couldn't pay it back—were lazy and wasteful. They did not see debtors as victims of misfortune or bad luck. In England and colonial America, failure to pay one's debts was considered a crime.

Debtors were often sent to prison as punishment. Like all prisoners of that era, debtors were expected to pay for their food and lodging while they sat in jail. They could starve unless their families brought them food. While locked up, debtors had no way to earn money and pay back what was owed. They might spend the rest of their lives behind bars, with no hope for release.

The laws concerning debt changed gradually. Instead of going to prison, some debtors were allowed to pay off their debts by working or by serving in the military. Debtors' prisons finally disappeared from England and the United States by the mid-1900s.

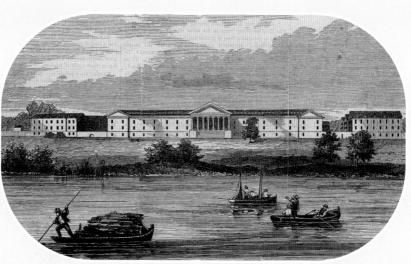

Chapter FOUR

Phillis Wheatley's Legacy

A pamphlet published by abolitionists

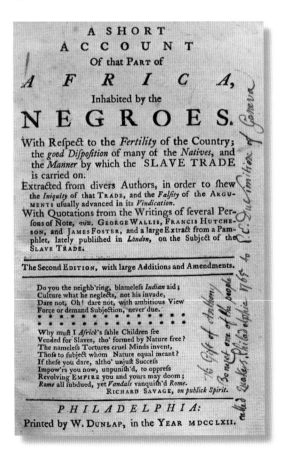

A SHORT
ACCOUNT
Of that PART of
A R I C *A,*
Inhabited by the
NEGROES.
With Respect to the *Fertility* of the Country; the *good Disposition* of many of the *Natives,* and the *Manner* by which the SLAVE TRADE is carried on.
Extracted from divers Authors, in order to shew the *Iniquity* of that TRADE, and the *Falsity* of the ARGUMENTS usually advanced in its *Vindication.*
With Quotations from the Writings of several Persons of Note, *viz.* GEORGE WALLIS, FRANCIS HUTCHESON, and JAMES FOSTER, and a large Extract from a Pamphlet, lately published in *London,* on the Subject of the SLAVE TRADE.

The Second EDITION, with large Additions and Amendments.

Do you the neighb'ring, blameless *Indian* aid ;
Culture what he neglects, not his invade,
Dare not, Oh! dare not, with ambitious View
Force or demand Subjection, never due.
• • • • • • • • • • • • • • •
Why must I *Africk's* sable Children see
Vended for Slaves, tho' formed by Nature free ?
The nameless Tortures cruel Minds invent,
Those to subject whom Nature equal meant ?
If these you dare, altho' unjust Success
Impow'rs you now, unpunish'd, to oppress
Revolving EMPIRE you and yours may doom ;
Rome all subdued, yet *Vandals* vanquish'd *Rome.*
RICHARD SAVAGE, on *publick Spirit.*

PHILADELPHIA:
Printed by W. DUNLAP, in the YEAR MDCCLXII.

IN THE EARLY 1770S, MANY PEOPLE IN ENGLAND and the British colonies had begun to argue that slavery was immoral. They pointed out that, according to Christian teachings, all humans are the children of God. It was wrong for one person to own his brother or sister as a piece of property. Those who favored slavery insisted that Africans were not equal to people of European heritage. They justified slavery by claiming that black people were less intelligent and less capable than whites. They sometimes quoted from the Bible to try to support their idea that slavery was the right thing to do.

Dinah Morris, a slave in the northern United States, is given her manumission papers

Phillis Wheatley's poems appeared in the midst of this debate. She proved that an African could become fully educated. She had mastered the poetic style popular among white poets of her time. Opponents of slavery liked to point out Wheatley's achievements. After reading Wheatley's poems, how could anyone say that Africans belonged to an **inferior** race?

Although Phillis Wheatley died in poverty, her work was never forgotten. *Poems on*

Copies of Wheatley's book on display at Old South Church in Boston

Various Subjects was reprinted five times in England between 1773 and 1820. During the same period, seven editions of the book appeared in the United States. In the 1830s, the movement to abolish, or end, slavery gained new strength. Abolitionist newspapers reprinted many of Wheatley's poems.

Wheatley's work attracted renewed interest in the 1960s. Some readers felt that Wheatley supported slavery in her poetry. They quoted her famous poem, "On Being Brought from Africa to America," which begins:

Twas mercy brought me from my pagan land
Taught my benighted soul to understand
That there's a God, that there's a savior too…

In these lines, Wheatley seems to be saying that she is grateful for her capture, because it led her to Christianity. But this poem also shows that Wheatley saw the black and white races as equal under God. She goes on to write:

Remember, Christians, Negroes black as Cain
May be refined, and join the angelic train.

Statue of Wheatley on display at Old South Meeting House in Boston

▶ Today, many schools and organizations in the United States are named in honor of Phillis Wheatley.

Phillis Wheatley is remembered as the first African-American poet.

© Elizabeth Catlett/Licensed by VAGA, New York, NY

Phillis Wheatley's experience of slavery had a profound impact upon her writing. Much of her work expresses a longing for what she called "fair freedom." In her thoughts about this world and the next, she imagined that freedom was "smiling like the morn."

Today Phillis Wheatley is regarded as the first African-American poet. She is also one of the first women writers in what is now the United States. Several schools and libraries have been named in her honor. Special museum exhibits have focused on her life and work. Scholars write articles about her poetry and her influence on literature and history.

Phillis Wheatley died at the age of 31. She published only one small book of poetry during her brief lifetime. Yet her work and her story left their mark on the history of the United States.

ca. 1753   Phillis Wheatley is born somewhere in West Africa, possibly in present-day Senegal.

1761   Phillis is captured by slave hunters and sold in Boston to John Wheatley.

1767   The first poem by Phillis Wheatley is published in a Rhode Island newspaper.

1772   Eighteen of Boston's leading citizens question Wheatley and agree that she is indeed the author of her poems.

1773   Wheatley goes to England and finds a London publisher for *Poems on Various Subjects, Religious and Moral.* Susannah Wheatley signs manumission papers making Wheatley a free woman.

1774   Wheatley writes a strong antislavery statement in a letter to preacher Samson Occom.

1775   The American Revolutionary War begins.

1776   The Declaration of Independence is signed on July 4.

1778   Wheatley marries John Peters, a free black man.

1783   The American Revolutionary War ends in victory for the United States of America.

1784   Wheatley dies in poverty.

fluently (FLOO-uhnt-lee)
Speaking a language fluently means that you speak it clearly and smoothly. Phillis Wheatley quickly learned to speak English fluently.

hoax (HOHKS)
A hoax is a carefully planned trick designed to mislead the public. Boston publishers thought Phillis Wheatley's poems were a hoax.

impostor (im-POSS-tur)
An impostor is a person who pretends to be something or someone he or she is not. The people of Boston wondered if Phillis Wheatley was an impostor.

inferior (in-FIHR-ee-ur)
If something is inferior, it is not as good as other things. In Phillis Wheatley's time, Africans were considered to be part of an inferior group of people.

manumission (MAN-you-mish-uhn)
Manumission is the act of formally releasing someone from slavery. Phillis Wheatley's owner signed manumission papers, which released Phillis from slavery in 1773.

manuscript (MAN-yuh-skript)
A manuscript is the author's unpublished copy of a poem, novel, story, etc. The manuscript of one of Phillis Wheatley's poems sold for $68,500.

myths (MITHS)
Myths are stories that explain a group's beliefs or that tell about gods and goddesses. Phillis Wheatley learned the myths of the ancient Greeks.

philosophy (fuh-LOSS-uh-fee)
A philosophy is a set of ideas that explain how the world works. Phillis Wheatley learned about Greek philosophy.

port of call (PORT UHV KAWL)
A port of call is a place where a ship stops for supplies, repairs, or to drop off or pick up cargo on its way to its final destination. The ship's first port of call was somewhere in the West Indies.

preface (PREF-iss)
A preface is an introduction to a book. Eighteen Boston residents wrote a preface for Phillis Wheatley's book of poems.

Web Sites

Visit our homepage for lots of links about Phillis Wheatley:
http://www.childsworld.com/links.html

Note to Parents, Teachers, and Librarians:
We routinely verify our Web links to make sure they're safe,
active sites—so encourage your readers to check them out!

Books

Lasky, Kathryn. *A Voice of Her Own: The Story of Phillis Wheatley, Slave Poet.*
Cambridge, Mass.: Candlewick Press, 2003.

Rinaldi, Ann. *Hang a Thousand Trees with Ribbons: The Story of Phillis Wheatley.*
New York: Harcourt, 1996.

Salisbury, Cynthia. *Phillis Wheatley: Legendary African-American Poet.* Berkeley
Heights, N.J.: Enslow, 2001.

Weidt, Maryann, and Mary O'Keefe Young (illustrator). *Revolutionary Poet: A
Story about Phillis Wheatley.* Minneapolis: Lerner Publications, 1997.

Places to Visit or Contact

The Bostonian Society
*To write for information about visiting the Phillis Wheatley landing site on the Boston
Women's Heritage Trail*
Old State House
206 Washington Street
Boston, MA 02109-1713
617/720-1713

The Anacostia Museum and Center for African American History and Culture
To visit and learn more about African-American history and culture
1901 Fort Place, S.E.
Washington, DC 20020
202/287-3306

31

Index

About the Author

DEBORAH KENT GREW UP IN LITTLE FALLS, NEW JERSEY, AND received her bachelor's degree from Oberlin College. She earned a master's degree from Smith College School for Social Work and worked as a social worker before becoming a full-time writer. She is the author of 18 young-adult novels and more than 50 nonfiction titles for children. She lives in Chicago with her husband, children's author R. Conrad Stein, and their daughter, Janna.